ALABAMA

in words and pictures

BY DENNIS B. FRADIN

ILLUSTRATIONS BY RICHARD WAHL

MAPS BY LEN W. MEENTS

Consultant:
Milo B. Howard, Jr.
Alabama Department of
Archives and History

 CHILDRENS PRESS, CHICAGO

For my Aunt, June Rachuy Brindel, who started me in writing children's books

For Their Help, the Author Thanks:
Milo B. Howard, Jr., Alabama Department of Archi
and History
Amos Crisp, Public Affairs Office, Marshall Space F
Center

Buck's Pocket State Park, Grove Oak

Library of Congress Cataloging in Publication Data

Fradin, Dennis B
  Alabama in words and pictures.

  SUMMARY: Presents a brief history and description
of the Heart of Dixie.
  1. Alabama—Juvenile literature.
[1. Alabama] I. Wahl, Richard, 1939-
II. Meents, Len W. III. Title.
F326.3.F72   976.1   80-15135
ISBN 0-516-03901-6

Picture Acknowledgments:
ALABAMA BUREAU OF PUBLICITY AND INFORMATION—Cover, 1, 4, 5,
11, 15 (right), 16, 19, 21, 25, 27 (bottom left), 29, 32, 33, 34, 35, 37, 38, 41
BIRMINGHAM AREA CHAMBER OF COMMERCE—15 (left), 23, 24
HUNTSVILLE CONVENTION AND VISITORS BUREAU—17, 27 (top left)
NASA—27 (right)
COVER—Azalea Trail Maids, Mobile

Alabama

Alabama (AL • uh • BAM • uh) was named after the Alibamu (AL • ih • BAM • oo) Indian tribe. The state is in the deep South. Over a hundred years ago, Alabama was a great cotton-growing state.

Alabama is still a leading cotton-growing state. But today, more Alabama people work in factories than on farms. Iron and steel are made in the state. Rockets that helped land people on the moon were made in Alabama. The state has much more. . . .

Do you know where the Confederate (kun • FED • er • it) capital was located at the start of the Civil War? Or where you can see a cave that was home to people 9,000 years ago? Do you know where the blind and deaf author, Helen Keller, was born? Or where baseball's home-run king, Henry Aaron (AIR • un), was born? As you will learn, the answer to these questions is: Alabama!

Millions of years ago, oceans covered Alabama. How do scientists know this? Fossils of sea life have been found on land that is now dry. In 1961, a farmer was plowing his field near Millry (MILL • ree). He dug up a whale skeleton! Sharks' teeth and fossils of sea turtles have also been found in Alabama.

The first people came to Alabama at least 9,000 years ago. Alabama has a cave where much has been learned about early people. It is Russell Cave, in northeast Alabama. At the bottom of the cave, remains of early fires have been dug up. The skeleton of a man who may have been murdered 3,000 years ago was found in Russell Cave. A spearhead was found near the bones of his spine.

Russell Cave National Monument, Bridgeport

Mound State Park, Moundville

The people who lived in the cave were not neat. As years passed, they just covered old things with dirt and went on living there.

Later, people moved out of caves and learned to farm. One group that lived in Alabama about 1,000 years ago is now called the *Mound Builders*. They grew corn. They also built big dirt hills, known as *mounds*. Some mounds were used bury the dead. Temples were built on top of other mounds. You can see the remains of a Mound Builders' town. It is at Moundville, in western Alabama. There are 34 mounds there.

In more recent times, a number of Indian tribes lived
in Alabama. The Cherokee (CHAIR • oh • kee) and the
Chickasaw (CHICK • uh • saw) lived in the north. The
Creek and the Choctaw (CHOCK • taw) were in the south.
The Seminole (SEM • i • nohl) and Alibamu were two
other tribes.

The Indians built villages. Some lived in wigwams,
which were round huts. Others lived in log houses. The
Indians farmed and hunted. Corn, pumpkins, and beans
were some of their crops. In those days the Alabama

woods were filled with deer, elk, and bears. The Indians hunted these animals with bows and arrows. The meat was food. The skins were used to make clothes.

The Indians had interesting customs. The Creek held their Green Corn Dance near harvesttime. It was their Thanksgiving. They thanked the gods for giving them food. The Indians also enjoyed sports. They played a ball game much like modern lacrosse (lah • CROSS). The ball was made of deerskin. The racquets and goals were made of wood.

The Cherokee, Chickasaw, Creek, Choctaw, and Seminole were later called the "Five Civilized Tribes" by white settlers. Settlers thought they had an advanced way of life.

The Spanish were the first known explorers in Alabama. They arrived in the early 1500s. The Spanish wanted gold. Some think Alonzo de Piñeda (ah • LON • zoh day pin • YAY • dah) was the first to enter Alabama.

It is known that the Spaniard De Soto (dih SO • toh) entered Alabama in 1540. While searching for gold, De Soto murdered many Indians. Chief Tuscaloosa (TUSS • kah • LOO • suh) was a Choctaw Indian who fought back. Tuscaloosa gathered thousands of Indians in his village at Maubila (maw • BEE • lah). The Indians had bows and arrows. But the Spaniards had guns and swords. The Indians lost this bloody battle, known as the Battle of Maubila. The Indians fought newcomers for many years after that.

One Spanish gold hunter, Tristán de Luna (TRISS • tan dih LOO • nah) tried to form settlements on Mobile (moh • BEEL) Bay in 1559. His people ran out of food and they left. The Spanish lost interest in Alabama because they did not find gold there.

The French built the first permanent settlement in Alabama. The French wanted to trade with the Indians for furs. They also wanted to rule as much land in America as they could. Two French brothers, the Le Moynes (lih MOIN), built Fort Louis (LOO • iss) on the Mobile River in 1702. There were floods, so they had to move. The new settlement, built in 1711, became the city of Mobile. French soldiers, farmers, and traders lived in Mobile. Today, Mobile is Alabama's oldest city.

The French built other settlements. Then from 1754 to 1763 France fought a war with England. England won. England took control of the region. But not for long!

In 1776 a new country was formed in America. It was called the United States of America. The United States wanted Alabama. In 1783 much of Alabama passed from England to the United States. But the Indians still fought for their lands. The Creek fought from 1813 to 1814. General Andrew Jackson was sent to Alabama. In 1814, Jackson ended the Creek War at the Battle of Horseshoe Bend. The Creek lost and had to give up their lands in Alabama.

In 1817 Alabama became a territory. It wasn't a state yet. It was land owned by the United States.

Two years later, on December 14, 1819, Alabama became our 22nd state. Huntsville was the first state capital. It wasn't until 1846 that Montgomery (mont • GOM • ree) became the capital, as it is today.

Thousands of Americans moved into the new state. Many grew cotton. Cotton grows well where it is warm. It needs rich soil and good rainfall. Alabama was perfect. Some people had small cotton farms. Others had huge farms, called *plantations* (plan • TAY • shunz). Black slaves did the work of growing and picking cotton on the plantations.

The cotton was sent to factories in the North and in England. It was made into cloth and clothes. In the 1800s, many clothes were made of cotton.

Cotton was so important to the South that it was called "King Cotton." Alabama grew so much cotton that it was nicknamed the *Cotton State*. More and more slaves were brought to Alabama to work in the cotton fields. By 1860 almost half the people living in Alabama were slaves.

A cotton field

In the late 1850s, Americans argued over slavery. It looked like the United States government would soon end slavery. Southerners who grew cotton didn't want that to happen.

Southerners had other complaints. They sold much of their cotton to Europe. They also bought items from there. U.S. taxes, called *tariffs* (TAIR • ifs) made it costly for Southerners to buy from Europe. Southerners spoke of "States' Rights." They felt that each state should decide for itself about slavery, taxes, and other issues.

One by one, Southern states seceded (sih • SEE • ded) from (left) the United States. Alabama left the United States on January 11, 1861. Southerners met at Montgomery, Alabama. They formed their own country on February 8, 1861. They called it the Confederate States of America. Montgomery became known as the *Cradle of the Confederacy* because the Confederate States of America was formed there.

Two months later the Civil War (1861-1865) began. It

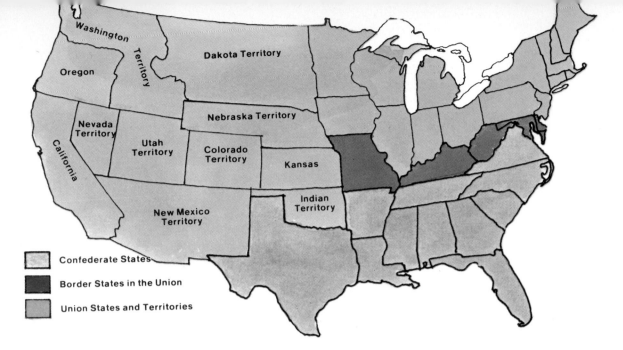

Confederate States

Border States in the Union

Union States and Territories

was fought between the Southern (or Confederate) states and the Northern (or Union) states. For four months in 1861 Montgomery served as the Confederate capital. The president of the Confederacy, Jefferson Davis, took office and lived in Montgomery.

Alabama sent about 100,000 men to fight in the Southern army. They fought in many states. The Battle of Mobile Bay in August of 1864 was one of the main Civil War battles in Alabama. Northern ships blocked the bay. Supplies could not get into Mobile. Northern soldiers took control of Mobile in April of 1865. That same month Northern soldiers burned the University of Alabama at Tuscaloosa.

13

The North had more soldiers. It had better supplies. By 1865 the North had won the Civil War. The slaves were freed in Alabama that same year.

The Civil War was the bloodiest war in our nation's history. As many as 70,000 Alabamians (al • ah • BAM • ee • yans) may have been killed or wounded in it. After the Civil War, much of Alabama was in ruin. Cities were wrecked. With slaves gone, the plantation system ended. People still farmed. Many were *tenant farmers*. These were people who rented land from big landowners. Whether black or white, most were very poor. What made things worse was that dishonest lawmakers from the North ran Alabama for about ten years.

Alabamians saw that they would have to rebuild their own state. They went to work. In the late 1800s manufacturing (making things) became important. Textile mills were built in the Chattahoochee Valley. In the mills cotton was made into cloth.

Left: An old steel-smelting Sloss furnace in downtown Birmingham. Although it is not used anymore, it has become a landmark.
Above: Smelting steel in a modern plant

There is a lot of coal in the Birmingham (BURR • ming • ham) area. There is iron ore. There is limestone. All these are needed to make iron and steel. Birmingham became a big iron and steel-making city. These metals are still made there today.

Alabamians looked around and saw that they had a kind of "green gold" in their state. Trees! Forests were cut. They became paper and other wood products.

Railroads were built through Alabama. In the early 1900s metals, wood products, and other Alabama products went by train to other cities in America.

The Tennessee (ten • nuh • SEE) River flows through northern Alabama. The valley of this river lies in seven states, including Alabama. In 1933 the United States formed the Tennessee Valley Authority (TVA). The TVA built dams on the river. Dams help keep the river from flooding. They also send water to farms when it is needed. This helps Alabama farmers grow many crops today. Wheeler Dam and Wilson Dam are two of the largest dams on the Tennessee River.

Wilson Dam

The Spaceship Lunar Odyssey at the Alabama Space and Rocket Center. "Astronauts" have buckled their seat belts for a simulated flight to the moon.

Dams also turn water power into electric power. This helps provide power for factories. Many factories have been built in the state. Metals, food, paper, and chemicals are leading products today.

One Alabama city helped put people in space. In 1960, the George C. Marshall Space Flight Center was formed at Huntsville. Rockets were designed there. Huntsville became known as *Rocket City, U. S. A.* The Saturn (SAT • ern) rocket that helped take the first men to the moon was designed in Huntsville.

If you think about Alabama's history, you can see how the state has been a battleground for many groups. De Soto and the Spanish fought Indians there. The French and the English fought for the land. The United States fought the Creek Indians to gain control. The Confederacy was formed in Alabama. Civil War battles were fought there.

In the 1950s and 1960s Alabama was again a battleground. This time the issue was civil rights. Although the slaves had been freed in 1865, blacks were still badly treated in many places in America. Sometimes they weren't allowed to vote. They were kept out of some jobs. They had to go to separate schools. A black Montgomery minister, Dr. Martin Luther King, Jr., worked to change that. He fought with words and marches. In 1965 he led a huge march from Selma (SELL • mah) to Montgomery. This helped get a law passed allowing more blacks to vote. Later, Dr. King moved to Atlanta, Georgia, where he had been born. He continued his civil rights work.

Today, Alabama lawmakers are working to improve life for all the state's citizens. They are working on the problems of older people. They are working to make better schools. They are working to keep the state's air and water clean.

You have learned about some of Alabama's history. Now it is time for a trip—in words and pictures— through the state.

De Soto Caverns

Alabama is shaped like a tall rectangle. Tennessee is the state to the north. Georgia is to the east. Florida and the body of water known as the Gulf of Mexico are to the south. The state of Mississippi (miss • a • SIP • ee) is to the west.

Pretend you are in an airplane high above Alabama. From the air, you see forests of pines and other trees. You see the Appalachian (ap • ah • LAISH • en) Mountains in the north. You see farms throughout the state. You see pretty blue rivers. Many—such as the Tennessee, Cahaba (ka • HA • buh), Tombigbee, Coosa, Tallapoosa (tahl • ah • POO • suh), and Alabama—have Indian names.

Your airplane is landing in a city on the Alabama River. This is Montgomery.

Once, Alibamu and Creek Indians lived here. Montgomery was founded as a town in 1817. It became a center for buying and selling cotton. Today, Montgomery is one of Alabama's biggest cities. It is also the capital of the state.

Left: State Capitol, Montgomery
Above: First White House of the Confederacy in Montgomery

Visit the state capitol building. This is where state lawmakers meet. Once, this building was the capitol of the Confederacy. Look for the brass star on the Capitol steps. That is where Jefferson Davis stood when he became president of the Confederacy.

Go to the First White House of the Confederacy. This was the home of President Jefferson Davis and his family while Montgomery was the Confederate capital. Later, Richmond, Virginia, was made the Confederate capital.

At the Archives and History Building you can learn about Indians and Civil War soldiers. Would you like to see what Montgomery looked like in the years before the Civil War? The city has old houses and museums where you can learn about those days gone by.

You can also see houses of modern people. Visit the Lurleen B. Wallace Memorial Museum. Lurleen B. Wallace was the only woman governor (from 1967 to 1968) of Alabama. Her husband, George C. Wallace, was a famous Alabama governor who served before and after her.

The famous civil rights leader, Martin Luther King, Jr., also lived in Montgomery. You can see the Dexter Avenue Baptist Church, where Dr. King served as pastor.

Today, furniture, glass, and paper are made in Montgomery. Since the city is Alabama's capital, many people work for the state government. You'll also see

The Birmingham skyline

many college students in Montgomery. Alabama State University and part of Auburn University are in the city.

If you go about 94 miles northwest of Montgomery you will come to Birmingham. This area was once home to Creek, Cherokee, and Choctaw Indians. The town was formed in 1871 as the meeting place of two railroads. Birmingham became a big iron and steel-making city. In the late 1800s and early 1900s, the United States needed these metals. They were used for making machines and buildings. Thousands came to work in Birmingham's steel mills. The city grew so fast that it was called the *Magic City*. Today, Birmingham is Alabama's biggest city.

Arlington

Iron and steel, chemicals and foods go by train or truck from Birmingham to other American cities.

Birmingham is in a lovely, hilly area. Go to the top of Red Mountain in Birmingham. The mountain is red from all the iron in it. There is a statue of Vulcan (VUL • kin) on top of Red Mountain. Vulcan was the Roman god of metal making. An elevator will take you high up inside the Vulcan monument.

There is much to remind you of the past in Birmingham. Visit Arlington Antebellum (ant • ee • BELL • um) Home and Gardens on Cotton Avenue. It was built in 1822.

The Birmingham Museum of Art, the Botanical Gardens, and the Birmingham Zoo also attract many visitors.

Statue of Vulcan in Birmingham

You'll see a lot of students in Birmingham. The University of Alabama in Birmingham is there. Did you ever hear of people having open-heart surgery? Many such operations are done at the Alabama Medical Center in Birmingham.

Northeast of Birmingham you will come to another of Alabama's biggest cities. This is Gadsden (GADZ • den). Steel is made there, too.

From Gadsden, head into northeast Alabama. You'll see mountains there. You'll see caves. You'll enjoy Sequoyah (sih • KWOI • yuh) Cave. It has weird rock formations. It also has lakes inside it. Saltpeter Cave and Russell Cave are also in northeast Alabama.

The Appalachian Mountains are in northern Alabama. In mountain areas, Alabamians have always had small farms. Mountain people planted their own crops. They built their own small houses. During the Civil War, some northern Alabamians tried to form their own state. It would have had no slavery. The great-great-grandchildren of these people still live on small farms in northern Alabama.

Huntsville is far up in northern Alabama. It is Alabama's fourth biggest city. Huntsville is called *Rocket City, U.S.A.* Many rockets and satellites have been designed at the Marshall Space Flight Center in Huntsville. Go visit the Alabama Space and Rocket Center. You will learn about rockets and space travel.

Top left: Downtown Huntsville
Bottom left: Alabama Space and Rocket Center
Below: The Space Shuttle, Marshall
Space Flight Center

After seeing Huntsville, head southwest towards Tuscaloosa. You'll pass through a large forest area. In all, about two-thirds of Alabama is covered by forests. Pines, cedars, and oaks grow well in Alabama. People enjoy the forests. So do animals. You might see deer in the forests. You might see foxes or even bobcats.

Tuscaloosa is about 150 miles southwest of Huntsville. The city was named after Chief Tuscaloosa. It lies on the Black Warrior River.

From 1826 to 1846, Tuscaloosa was the capital of Alabama. Today a section of Tuscaloosa is home to the University of Alabama. Students there study science, law, business, and other subjects. The school's football team is often one of the best in the country. Paul "Bear" Bryant became football coach of the University of Alabama in 1958. He is one of the most famous football coaches of all time.

South of Tuscaloosa you will come to an area known as the *Black Belt*. It has that name because of its fine black

Gaineswood

soils. Once, this was a great cotton-growing area. Huge

plantations were built here. You can still visit some

plantation houses here and elsewhere in Alabama. Bluff

Hall and Gaineswood are just two of them.

You'll still see cotton growing in Alabama. But it is no

longer Alabama's leading crop. Many different crops are

raised in Alabama today. In fact, you could eat very well on Alabama farm products. Beef cattle are raised for meat. Other cows are raised for milk. Hogs and chickens are raised by farmers. Soybeans are the leading crop. Corn, peanuts, pecans, peaches, pears, and strawberries are some other crops grown today.

Auburn University at Auburn is very important to Alabama farmers. This school teaches farmers how to keep their crops and animals healthy. The school maintains 23,000 acres throughout Alabama. On this land scientists work on new and better farming methods.

Alabama is still sometimes called the *Cotton State*. But Alabama has other nicknames now. During the Civil War, Alabama soldiers put yellow cloth on their uniforms. They looked like birds called yellowhammers. Today, the yellowhammer is the state bird and Alabama is often called the *Yellowhammer State*. The southern states are sometimes called *Dixie*. Since Alabama is in the middle of the South—and is important to southern history—the state is often called the *Heart of Dixie*.

As you go farther south in Alabama you may notice that it's getting warmer. In January, it is often 60° in southern Alabama. Some Alabama children have never seen snow!

Warm weather helps Alabama bloom with flowers in every season. The state is filled with lovely—and sweet-smelling—magnolias (mag • NOHL • yuhs), camellias (cah • MEEL • yuhs), and other flowers. Alligators also like Alabama's warm weather. You can see them in some

Fort Conde, Mobile

swampy areas of southern Alabama. If you see one, don't pet it! Their teeth are very sharp and their jaws are strong.

Mobile is near the southwest corner of the state. The city lies on the Mobile River where it flows into Mobile Bay. Mobile is Alabama's oldest city. It was founded here in 1711 by the French. In the 1800s, cotton was bought and sold in Mobile. The city lies near the Gulf of Mexico. Boats took cotton from Mobile to cities in Europe.

Today, Mobile is Alabama's second biggest city. It is still a seaport city. Boats take paper, clothes, and other Mobile products to many other cities.

Visit the battleship U.S.S. *Alabama* in Mobile Bay. This battleship served in World War II. It was about to be junked by the Navy. Governor George Wallace wanted to save it. Alabama schoolchildren gave nickels and dimes to pay for having the ship moved from Seattle to Mobile.

Battleship U.S.S. *Alabama*

Above: The Japanese Gardens at Birmingham
Botanical Gardens
Right: Beach at Gulf Shores

Visit Oakleigh (OAK • lee) in Mobile. Slaves built this
fancy house for a cotton merchant in the 1830s.

Mobile is famed for its lovely gardens. One of
Alabama's loveliest places is Bellingrath (BELL • in •
grath) Gardens and Home, a few miles south of Mobile.
This garden is a wonderland of color and sweet smells.

Alabama's southwest edge lies along the Gulf of Mexico.
Finish your Alabama trip by visiting the Gulf of Mexico
area. You'll see sandy beaches. Off the coast there are
islands, such as Dauphin (DAW • fin) Island. Once, pirate

Above: Blessing of the shrimp fleet,
Bayou La Batre
Left: A rich catch of red snappers,
crabs, and shrimp

ships lurked in this area. There are stories that the
pirate Jean Laffite (ZHAHN la • FEET) buried treasure
somewhere near Dauphin Island. Today, you won't see
pirate ships in the Gulf of Mexico. But you will see
fishing boats. Oysters, shrimp, red snappers, and crabs
are some of the seafoods caught in the Gulf.

Did you ever hear of big storms known as *hurricanes?* They sometimes strike southwest Alabama. In September of 1979 Hurricane Frederic (nicknamed Freddy) hit Mobile and the south Alabama area. Great damage was done.

Places can't tell the whole story of Alabama. Many interesting people have lived in the state.

John Pelham (PELL • em) was one of Alabama's great Civil War heroes. He was born in what is now Calhoun County, in 1838. He was just 24 years old when he became a major. The "Boy Major" became famous for his use of cannons in Civil War battles. He was not yet 25 years old when he was killed in 1863.

Raphael Semmes (RAFF • eye • ell SEMZ) was born in Maryland in 1809. He moved to Mobile and worked as a lawyer. During the Civil War, Semmes became captain of the *Alabama.* This ship, the *Alabama,* sank or captured over 60 Northern ships.

Helen Keller was born near Tuscumbia, Alabama, in 1880. When she was only a year and a half old she got sick. After that, she couldn't see. She couldn't hear. With her teacher's help, Helen learned to spell words by making signs with her fingers. She put her hands on people's faces when they spoke. Then she copied the way their mouths moved. She learned to speak that way. Helen Keller went to college. She wrote books. She proved that handicapped people can do a lot—if they get a chance.

Helen Keller's cottage in Tuscumbia

Trees covered with Spanish moss tower over a house near the fishing village of Bon Secour, famous for its oysters.

You already know that Martin Luther King, Jr. lived in Alabama. Other great black leaders have lived in the state. Booker T. Washington (1856-1915) founded a school for black people in Tuskegee (tuss • KEE • ghee). It is called Tuskegee Institute. The great black scientist, George Washington Carver (1859?-1943) worked and taught there. Carver was known as the "plant doctor." He made over 300 products from peanuts, including ink and soap.

Rosa Parks was born in Tuskegee in 1913. She didn't like the law that blacks in Montgomery had to sit in the back of buses. In 1955 she refused to move to the back of a bus. She was arrested. People protested. The law was then changed so that blacks could sit where they wanted.

Alabama has also produced some great sports figures. Did you ever hear of the boxer Joe Louis? He was born in a one-room shack in the cotton fields of Lafayette (LA • fay • et), Alabama, in 1914. The "Brown Bomber" held the heavyweight title longer than any other man—12 years. Jesse Owens was a great runner who was born in Danville, Alabama in 1913. He won four gold medals in the 1936 Olympic Games.

Henry Aaron was born in Mobile, Alabama, in 1934. He became a great baseball player. Aaron holds the all-time record for home runs—755. Another great baseball player, Willie Mays, was born in Fairfield, Alabama.

Alabama is also a very musical state. A black composer named W.C. Handy (1873-1958) created a new kind of music—the "blues." You can see the home where the "Father of the Blues" was born and raised, in Florence. Some well-known singers were born in Alabama. Nat King Cole and Hank Williams, Sr. are two of the names you may have heard. Tammy Wynette was born on a farm that was partly in Mississippi and partly in Alabama.

Home to the ancient people of Russell Cave . . . Mound Builders . . . Creek Indians . . . and cotton planters.

Top left: Alabama International Motor Speedway, Talladega
Bottom left: Ave Maria Grotto, Cullman
Above: Cheaha State Park, Lineville

Later a home to the "Boy Major" ... Helen Keller

... Dr. Martin Luther King, Jr. ... and Henry Aaron.

Once a big cotton-growing state...

Today a state where rockets and steel are made...

This is Alabama—the Heart of Dixie!

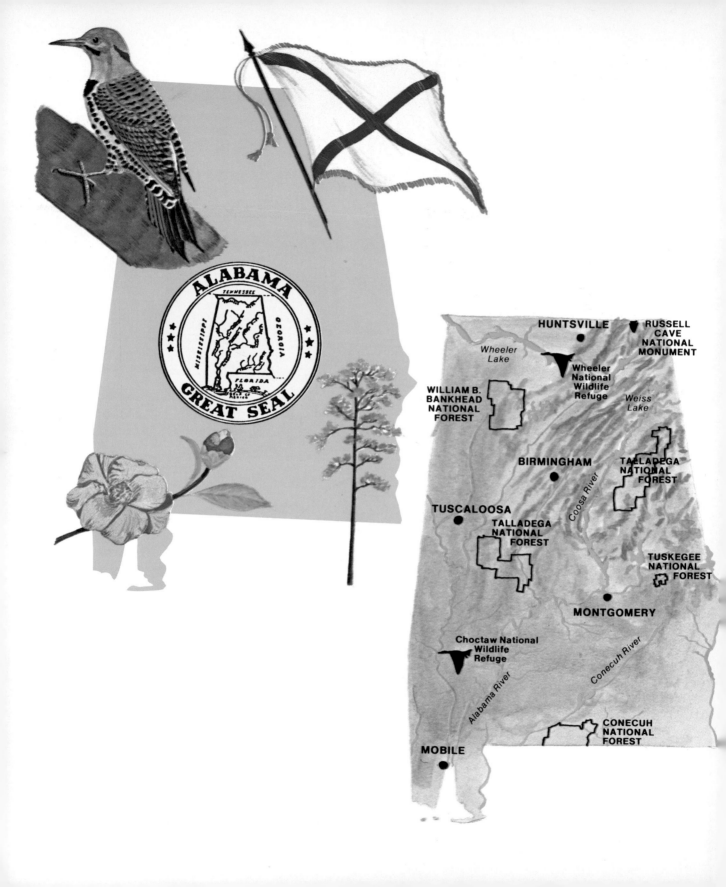

ALABAMA

GREAT SEAL

TENNESSEE

MISSISSIPPI GEORGIA

FLORIDA

SEAL OF ALABAMA

HUNTSVILLE

RUSSELL CAVE NATIONAL MONUMENT

Wheeler Lake

Wheeler National Wildlife Refuge

Weiss Lake

WILLIAM B. BANKHEAD NATIONAL FOREST

BIRMINGHAM

Coosa River

TALLADEGA NATIONAL FOREST

TUSCALOOSA

TALLADEGA NATIONAL FOREST

TUSKEGEE NATIONAL FOREST

MONTGOMERY

Choctaw National Wildlife Refuge

Conecuh River

Alabama River

CONECUH NATIONAL FOREST

MOBILE

Facts About ALABAMA

Area—51,609 square miles (29th biggest state)

Greatest Distance North to South—331 miles

Greatest Distance East to West—207 miles

Borders—Tennessee to the north; Georgia to the east, partly across the
Chattahoochee River; Florida and the Gulf of Mexico to the south;
Mississippi to the west

Highest Point—2,407 feet above sea level (Cheaha Mountain)

Lowest Point—Sea level, at the Gulf of Mexico

Hottest Recorded Temperature—112° (at Centreville on September 5, 1925)

Coldest Recorded Temperature—Minus 24° (at Russellville on January 31,
1966)

Statehood—Our 22nd state, on December 14, 1819

Origin of Name Alabama—The state was named for the Alibamu Indians;
Alibamu is thought to mean "thicket clearers" or "vegetation gatherers"

Capital—Montgomery (1846)

Previous Capitals—St. Stephens (territorial), Huntsville, Cahaba, and
Tuscaloosa

Counties—67

U.S. Senators—2

U.S. Representatives—7

State Senators—35

State Representatives—105

State Song—"Alabama" by Julia S. Tutwiler and Edna Goeckel Gussen

State Motto—*Audemus jura nostra defendere* (Latin meaning "We dare defend
our rights.")

Nicknames—The Heart of Dixie, the Yellowhammer State, the Cotton State

State Seal—First used in 1819

State Flag—Adopted in 1895

State Flower—Camellia

State Bird—Yellowhammer

State Fish—Fighting tarpon

State Tree—Southern pine

Some Rivers—Alabama, Tombigbee, Mobile, Black Warrior, Sipsey, Cahaba,
Coosa, Tallapoosa, Little Tallapoosa, Tennessee

Largest Lake—Guntersville Lake (man-made)

State Parks—21

National Forests—4

Wildlife—Rabbits, squirrels, deer, bobcats, foxes, minks, opossums, raccoons,
otters, beavers, skunks, turtles, alligators, rattlesnakes, cottonmouth
moccasins, coral snakes, wild turkeys, quail, ducks, geese, owls,
mockingbirds, yellowhammers, many other kinds of birds

Fishing—Shrimp, crab, oysters, red snapper, croakers, mussel shells, catfish,
buffalo fish, bream, tarpon, mullet, mackerel, flounder, bass, perch

Farm Products—Broiler chickens, eggs, milk, hogs, beef cattle, soybeans, wheat, hay, oats, potatoes, peanuts, pecans, cotton, strawberries, peaches, pears, tomatoes, sweet corn, watermelons

Mining—Coal, oil, natural gas, limestone, bauxite, marble

Manufacturing Products—Metals (iron, steel, and aluminum), many metal products, paper and paper products, many kinds of food products, chemicals, clothes, rubber products, plastic products, textiles

Population—3,690,000 (1977 estimate)

Major Cities—		
Birmingham	278,000	(all 1979 estimates)
Mobile	212,600	
Montgomery	161,400	
Huntsville	138,000	
Tuscaloosa	70,100	
Gadsden	48,500	
Dothan	46,600	

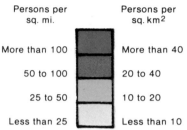

Persons per sq. mi.	Persons per sq. km²
More than 100	More than 40
50 to 100	20 to 40
25 to 50	10 to 20
Less than 25	Less than 10

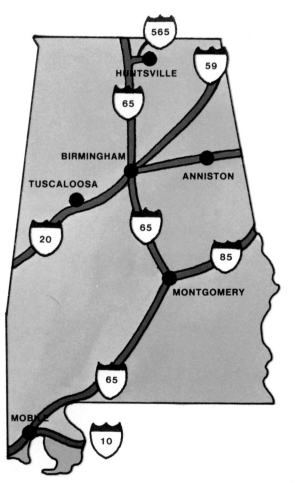

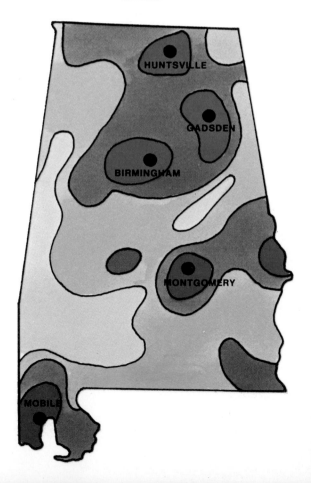

Alabama History

There have been people in Alabama for at least 9,000 years, and probably much longer.

1519—Spaniard Alonzo de Piñeda is thought to have entered Mobile Bay in this year

1528—Spaniard Panfilo de Narvaez enters Mobile Bay

1540—Spaniard De Soto explores what is now Alabama; in the Battle of Maubila, the Spanish kill thousands of Indians

1559—Tristán de Luna forms Spanish settlements on Mobile Bay, but they don't last

1702—Under the Le Moyne brothers, Frenchmen establish Fort Louis on the Mobile River

1711—Because of floods, the French colony moves to where the city of Mobile now stands; Mobile is the first permanent non-Indian town in Alabama

1719—Slaves are first brought to Alabama

1763—England takes control of Alabama area

1783—Much of Alabama passes from England into United States' control; but the Mobile Bay area belongs to Spain

1813—United States takes control of Mobile Bay area from Spain

1814—After Andrew Jackson and U.S. soldiers beat the Creek in the Battle of Horseshoe Bend, the Indians give up their Alabama lands

1817—Alabama Territory is formed

1819—On December 14, Alabama becomes our 22nd state; Huntsville is the capital

1820—Population of the new state is 127,901

1831—University of Alabama opens; in this same year the first railroad is begun in the state

1833—Meteor shower over Alabama; Alabamians call this "the year the stars fell"

1846—Montgomery becomes the state capital

1854—Public school system established in Alabama

1860—About 526,400 whites, 435,100 black slaves, and 2,700 free blacks live in Alabama

1861—On January 11, Alabama secedes from the United States; on February 4 southerners meet in Montgomery; on February 8, the Confederate States of America is formed, in Montgomery, with Montgomery the capital; the Civil War begins on April 12

1865—Civil War ends, leaving much of Alabama in ruins; as many as 100,000 Alabama men fought in the Civil War, with as many as 70,000 killed; in this same year Alabama's slaves are freed

1868—On June 25, Alabama is readmitted to the United States

1871—Birmingham is founded

1880—First blast furnace for making iron is built in Birmingham; the city soon becomes a great iron and steel-making center

1900—Population of Alabama is 1,828,697

1901—The present state constitution is adopted

1914-1918—During World War I, about 87,000 Alabamians fight for U.S.; the state produces food, cotton, and ships for the war effort

1929—Huge floods in southern Alabama

1933—Tennessee Valley Authority (TVA) is created, bringing flood control and new electric power to Alabama

1939-1945—During World War II, over 288,000 Alabama men and women are in service; at the Redstone Arsenal at Huntsville, work begins on developing rockets during the war

1953—Russell Cave is discovered in northeast Alabama

1956—Court order is made to end segregation on Montgomery buses

1960—The George C. Marshall Space Flight Center is founded at Huntsville

1962—George C. Wallace, born in Clio, Alabama, is elected governor

1965—Montgomery minister Dr. Martin Luther King, Jr. leads big "march" from Selma to Montgomery; this leads to law allowing more Alabama blacks to vote

1966—Lurleen Wallace is elected Alabama's first woman governor

1968—On April 4 Dr. Martin Luther King, Jr. is shot and killed in Tennessee; on May 7 Governor Lurleen Wallace dies of cancer; in this same year George C. Wallace runs for president, gets about 10 million votes, but loses

1970—Population of Alabama is 3,444,165

1971—Alabama passes laws to stop pollution

1972—Governor George Wallace is shot and wounded while in Maryland; it leaves him paralyzed

1973—Birmingham Municipal Airport is enlarged

1974—George Wallace is first Alabama governor to be elected for three terms

1977—Tornadoes kill more than 20 people in the state

1978—Forrest H. "Fob" James, Jr. is elected the state's 51st governor

1979—Hurricane Frederic devastates Mobile area.

INDEX

INDEX, Cont'd

About the Author:

Dennis Fradin attended Northwestern University on a creative writing scholarship and graduated in 1967. While still at Northwestern, he published his first stories in *Ingenue* magazine and also won a prize in *Seventeen's* short story competition. A prolific writer, Dennis Fradin has been regularly publishing stories in such diverse places as *The Saturday Evening Post, Scholastic, National Humane Review, Midwest,* and *The Teaching Paper.* He has also scripted several educational films. Since 1970 he has taught second grade reading in a Chicago school—a rewarding job, which, the author says, "provides a captive audience on whom I test my children's stories." Married and the father of three children, Dennis Fradin spends his free time with his family or playing a myriad of sports and games with his childhood chums.

About the Artists:

Len Meents studied painting and drawing at Southern Illinois University and after graduation in 1969 he moved to Chicago. Mr. Meents works full time as a painter and illustrator. He and his wife and child currently make their home in LaGrange, Illinois.

Richard Wahl, graduate of the Art Center College of Design in Los Angeles, has illustrated a number of magazine articles and booklets. He is a skilled artist and photographer who advocates realistic interpretations of his subjects. He lives with his wife and two sons in Libertyville, Illinois.